# Growing Your Business Without Breaking the Bank

*Proven Strategies for Maximizing Growth on a Budget for all Businesses*

*Written By*

Bamidele Iseoluwa Nathaniel

# TABLE OF CONTENTS

To God Almighty, who is the source of all wisdom and knowledge, I wholeheartedly dedicate this book, "Growing Your Business Without Breaking the Bank." Without His grace, this book would not have come to fruition.

I also dedicate this book to all the entrepreneurs who are struggling to grow their businesses due to financial constraints. May the strategies and insights in this book serve as a guiding light for you, empowering you to scale your business without breaking the bank.

Lastly, I dedicate this book to my family, friends, and colleagues, who have provided unwavering support and encouragement throughout my journey as an entrepreneur and author. Thank you for believing in me and for inspiring me to pursue my dreams.

## Acknowledgments

I would like to express my heartfelt gratitude to my parents, Daddy and Mummy Oyelowo, for their unwavering support and encouragement throughout my life. Your love and guidance have been invaluable to me, and I am forever grateful.

I also want to acknowledge my Pastor, Pastor Bosun Sonuyi, for his spiritual guidance and teachings, which have shaped me into the person I am today.

A special thanks to my editor, Priyanka Gupta, for your exceptional work and dedication to ensuring this book meets the highest standards. Your keen eye for detail and constructive criticism have been invaluable to the completion of this project.

I would also like to thank my uncles, Dami and Victor Oyelowo, and my aunt, Toluwa, for your support and encouragement throughout my journey. Your belief in me has been a constant source of motivation.

To my mentors, friends, and business partners, I am forever grateful for your guidance, support, and encouragement. Your invaluable advice and insights have helped me navigate the challenges of entrepreneurship.

Finally, I want to express my sincere gratitude to everyone who has contributed to this book in one way or another. Your contributions, whether big or small, have helped shape this project into what it is today. Thank you all.

## Foreword

As an entrepreneur myself, I know how challenging it can be to start and grow a business, especially when finances are limited. However, I also know that with the right knowledge, tools, and mindset, it is possible to achieve success without breaking the bank.

That is why I am honored to write the foreword for "Growing Your Business Without Breaking the Bank." This book is a comprehensive guide that provides practical strategies and advice for entrepreneurs who want to start and grow their business on a budget.

The author's passion for entrepreneurship and dedication to helping others succeed is evident in every chapter of this book. From identifying the right business idea to managing finances and hiring employees, the author provides valuable insights and practical tips that are easy to implement.

I commend the author for putting together such a valuable resource, and I believe that this book will be a game-changer for anyone who wants to grow their business without breaking the bank. I encourage every entrepreneur, whether just starting or already established, to read this book and apply the knowledge and strategies outlined within its pages.

Congratulations to the author for a job well done.

Best regards,

**Harsh Khandelwal**

*Founder of Waplia Digial Solutions (Private Limited Company India)*

# Introduction:

As an entrepreneur or business owner, you understand the importance of growing your business to remain competitive and successful. However, the process of expanding your business can be challenging, particularly when it comes to managing the financial aspect of growth. Breaking the bank to fund business growth is a common mistake that can lead to financial instability or failure.

This is where this book, "Growing Your Business Without Breaking the Bank," comes in. In this book, we provide a practical guide to help you grow your business without overspending or sacrificing your financial stability. We will share effective strategies, insights, and tools that will help you assess your current financial status, develop a growth plan, market and promote your business, streamline your operations, and finance your growth, all while managing your finances effectively.

With this book, you will learn how to make informed decisions, optimize resources, and maximize efficiency to grow your business on a budget. Whether you are a small business owner, an entrepreneur, or a startup founder, this book will provide valuable tips and guidance to help you achieve your growth goals and take your business to the next level.

# CHAPTER I

## The importance of growing a business without overspending

Growing a business is crucial for long-term success, but it can also be expensive. Overspending during the growth process can lead to financial instability or even business failure. This is why it's important to focus on growing your business without overspending.

One of the primary reasons to avoid overspending during growth is to maintain financial stability. Overspending can quickly lead to cash flow problems and may result in business owners taking on too much debt. This can make it difficult to manage day-to-day operations, and it may limit your ability to invest in future growth.

In addition to financial stability, growing your business without overspending can also help you make better business decisions. When you're forced to work within a budget, you become more strategic in your approach. You're forced to consider every dollar or naira spent and to prioritize your expenses based on their potential return on investment.

Finally, growing your business without overspending can also help you stay competitive in the market. By being mindful of your spending, you can keep your prices competitive, which can help you attract new customers and retain existing ones. It also allows you to invest in new products, services, or technology that can help you stay ahead of your competitors.

In conclusion, growing your business without overspending is critical for long-term success. It allows you to maintain financial stability, make better business decisions, and stay competitive in the market. By following the strategies outlined in this book, you can grow your business while keeping your expenses in check, and position yourself for continued success.

## Overview of the book's content

"Growing Your Business Without Breaking the Bank" is a comprehensive guide that addresses the challenges of growing a business on a budget. The book is divided into ten chapters that cover various aspects of business growth while keeping the financial stability intact.

Chapter one emphasizes the importance of growing a business without overspending. It highlights how overspending can lead to financial instability, hindering the growth of a business. Chapter two is about assessing your current finances. It covers evaluating your financial situation, analyzing revenue, expenses, and profit margins, and identifying areas for improvement.

Chapter three discusses creating a budget, highlighting its importance, and providing strategies for reducing expenses. Chapter four is about marketing on a budget and leveraging social media and other digital platforms to reach a wider audience.

Chapter five addresses maximizing efficiency by streamlining operations, implementing technology to increase efficiency, and deciding between outsourcing vs. hiring in-house. Chapter six covers identifying financing options, pros and cons of different funding sources, and preparing a strong funding application.

Chapter seven focuses on scaling and growth, preparing for growth, strategies for scaling your business while maintaining financial stability, and avoiding common mistakes. Chapter eight discusses managing your business finances, developing a budget, managing cash flow, and utilizing financing options.

Chapter nine covers hiring and managing employees, including when to hire employees, tips for managing employees, and cost-effective ways to hire. Finally, chapter ten is a summary of the key points covered in the book, encouragement to take action, and final thoughts on growing a business without breaking the bank.

This book provides a practical and actionable approach to growing a business on a budget. The content is well-researched, insightful, and presents strategies that any entrepreneur can implement to achieve financial stability while scaling their business.

Challenges of growing a business on a budget

Growing a business on a budget can be a challenging endeavor. Limited financial resources often require entrepreneurs to be creative and resourceful in their approach to growing their business. One of the main challenges of growing a business on a budget is the need to balance growth with financial stability. While rapid growth can be enticing, it can also put a strain on a business's finances, leading to cash flow problems and potentially even bankruptcy.

Another challenge of growing a business on a budget is the need to prioritize investments. With limited financial resources, entrepreneurs must carefully choose which areas of the business to invest in, weighing the potential returns against the costs. This can be a difficult decision, as investing too much in one area of the business may leave other areas neglected.

Additionally, growing a business on a budget requires a high level of discipline and financial management skills. Entrepreneurs must be able to track their expenses, manage their cash flow, and make strategic decisions that maximize their return on investment. This can be especially challenging for those who are not familiar with financial management or do not have access to professional accounting services.

Overall, growing a business on a budget requires a unique set of skills and a willingness to be creative and resourceful in finding ways to drive growth while maintaining financial stability. While it may present challenges, it is possible to grow a successful business without overspending, and the rewards can be significant for those who are able to achieve this goal.

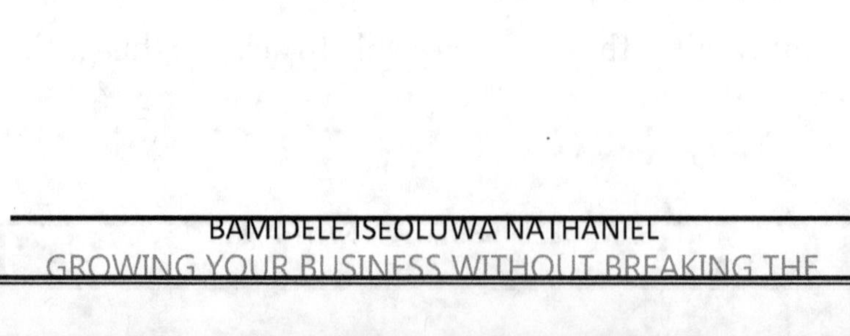

# CHAPTER II

## Assessing Your Current Finances

Assessing your current finances is a crucial step in growing your business without overspending. By taking a close look at your financial situation, you can identify areas where you may be overspending or where you may need to invest more money to achieve growth. In this chapter, we will cover the following topics:

1. Evaluating your financial situation

2. Analyzing revenue, expenses, and profit margins

3. Identifying areas for improvement

### 1. Evaluating Your Financial Situation

The first step in assessing your current finances is to evaluate your overall financial situation. This includes reviewing your financial statements such as your balance sheet, income statement, and cash flow statement. These documents will provide you with a clear picture of your financial standing, including your assets, liabilities, revenues, and expenses.

When evaluating your financial situation, consider factors such as your debt-to-equity ratio, your liquidity ratio, and your profitability. These financial metrics will help you understand your business's financial health and whether you are in a position to grow.

2. Analyzing Revenue, Expenses, and Profit Margins

After evaluating your financial situation, the next step is to analyze your revenue, expenses, and profit margins. This will help you understand where your money is coming from and where it's going. Review your sales and revenue figures and identify any trends or patterns. Look for areas where you could potentially increase revenue or cut expenses.

To analyze your expenses, categorize them by fixed and variable costs. Fixed costs are expenses that remain the same regardless of the level of sales, such as rent and salaries. Variable costs, on the other hand, are expenses that change based on the level of sales, such as inventory and marketing expenses. By identifying your fixed and variable costs, you can better understand your cost structure and identify areas where you may be overspending.

3.  Identifying Areas for Improvement

After evaluating your financial situation and analyzing your revenue, expenses, and profit margins, the final step is to identify areas for improvement. This may include reducing expenses, increasing revenue, or improving profitability. Look for areas where you can cut costs without sacrificing quality or customer service. Consider investing in areas where you can achieve a high return on investment, such as marketing or technology.

In conclusion, assessing your current finances is a critical step in growing your business without overspending. By evaluating your financial situation, analyzing your revenue, expenses, and profit margins, and identifying areas for improvement, you can develop a sound financial strategy that will help you

achieve your growth goals.


## Evaluating your financial situation

Evaluating your financial situation is an essential step towards growing your business without overspending. This involves assessing your current financial position, which includes understanding your revenue, expenses, and profit margins.

To evaluate your financial situation, you should first gather all your financial records, including bank statements, income statements, and balance sheets. This will give you a clear overview of your business's financial health, and you can then use this information to make informed decisions.

Next, you need to analyze your revenue streams. It's important to understand which products or services generate the most revenue for your business. You should also identify any trends or patterns in your sales figures, which will help you make more accurate revenue projections.

After analyzing your revenue streams, you should evaluate your expenses. This includes fixed and variable costs such as rent, utilities, employee salaries, and marketing expenses. Identify areas where you can reduce costs without negatively impacting the quality of your products or services. For instance, you can consider switching to more cost-effective suppliers, reducing your office space, or implementing energy-efficient practices to lower your utility bills.

Finally, you need to calculate your profit margins. This will give you a better understanding of how much profit you're making from each sale. It's important to keep track of your profit margins regularly to ensure that you're making a profit and that your business is sustainable.

Overall, evaluating your financial situation is crucial to growing your business without overspending. By understanding your revenue, expenses, and profit margins, you can make informed decisions about budgeting, marketing, and financing that will help your business thrive.

## Analyzing revenue, expenses, and profit margins

Once you have a clear understanding of your current financial situation, the next step is to analyze your revenue, expenses, and profit margins. This will help you identify areas where you can cut costs and increase revenue.

Revenue refers to the money coming into your business. You should analyze your revenue by looking at the sources of income for your business. This will help you determine which products or services are the most profitable and which ones are not generating enough revenue.

Expenses, on the other hand, refer to the money going out of your business. You should analyze your expenses by categorizing them into fixed and variable costs. Fixed costs are expenses that remain the same regardless of how much your business produces or sells, while variable costs are expenses that change depending on your business's level of production or sales.

Once you have identified your fixed and variable costs, you should analyze them to see where you can cut costs. For example, you may be able to negotiate better rates with your suppliers or find more cost-effective ways to market your products or services.

Profit margin refers to the percentage of revenue that is left over after you deduct all your expenses. Analyzing your profit margin will help you determine how much profit you are making on each sale. This can help you identify areas where you can increase your profit margin, such as by reducing your costs or increasing your prices.

Overall, analyzing your revenue, expenses, and profit margins is crucial to understanding the financial health of your business. It can help you make informed decisions about where to focus your efforts to grow your business while managing your budget effectively.

## Identifying areas for improvement

After evaluating your financial situation and analyzing your revenue, expenses, and profit margins, it's important to identify areas for improvement. This involves taking a closer look at your business operations and pinpointing specific areas where you can cut costs or increase revenue.

One way to identify areas for improvement is to conduct a SWOT analysis (Strengths, Weaknesses, Opportunities, and Threats). This analysis can help you identify areas where you excel and areas that need improvement. For example, you may have identified that your business has a strong online presence, but your in-store sales could use improvement.

Another approach is to conduct a thorough review of your expenses. This may involve looking at each expense category and determining if it is necessary or if there are ways to reduce the cost. For example, you may find that your business is spending too much on office supplies or utilities, and you can negotiate better rates or find more cost-effective alternatives.

In addition, you can also look for opportunities to increase revenue. This may involve expanding your product or service offerings, entering new markets, or finding new ways to sell to your existing customer base. For example, if you own a bakery, you may decide to offer catering services or partner with local cafes to sell your baked goods.

By identifying areas for improvement, you can create a plan of action to address these areas and improve your financial situation. This can help you grow your business without overspending and achieve long-term success.

# CHAPTER III

## Creating a Budget

Creating a budget is a crucial step towards growing a business without overspending. A budget helps you to plan and allocate your financial resources effectively. In this chapter, we will explore the importance of budgeting, how to create a realistic budget plan, and strategies for reducing expenses.

**Importance of Budgeting**

A budget provides a clear picture of your business's financial health. It helps you to identify areas where you need to cut costs and areas where you can invest more. A budget also allows you to set financial goals and track your progress towards achieving them. Without a budget, it is easy to overspend, which can lead to financial problems and hinder growth.

**Creating a Realistic Budget Plan**

Creating a realistic budget plan involves estimating your revenue and expenses for the upcoming period. You can start by reviewing your previous financial statements and identifying your average monthly revenue and expenses. Use this information to estimate your revenue and expenses for the upcoming period.

When creating a budget plan, it is essential to be realistic and consider all possible expenses. Remember to account for unexpected expenses such as repairs, maintenance, or legal fees. It is also important to set aside funds for emergencies and savings.

**Strategies for Reducing Expenses**

Reducing expenses is a key component of creating a budget plan. Here are some strategies for reducing expenses:

1.  Negotiate with suppliers: Negotiating with your suppliers can help you get better deals and lower prices.

2.  Cut unnecessary expenses: Review your expenses and identify areas where you can cut costs without affecting the quality of your products or services. This could include reducing office space or switching to a cheaper internet provider.

3.  Look for alternative financing options: Explore alternative financing options such as

crowdfunding, grants, or loans with lower interest rates.

4.  Automate processes: Automating processes can help you save time and reduce costs. Consider using automation tools for tasks such as invoicing or inventory management.

Creating a budget is a critical step towards growing your business without overspending. It allows you to plan and allocate your financial resources effectively, set financial goals, and track your progress. By creating a realistic budget plan and reducing expenses, you can improve your financial health and achieve your growth objectives.

Once you have a clear picture of your income and expenses, it's time to create a budget. A budget is essentially a financial plan that outlines your expected income and expenses over a set period of time, typically a month or a year. By creating a budget, you can gain better control over your finances and ensure that you are not overspending.

When creating a budget, it's important to be realistic and to take into account all of your expenses, including both fixed and variable costs. Fixed costs are expenses that stay the same from month to month, such as rent, loan payments, and insurance premiums. Variable costs, on the other hand, are expenses that can vary from month to month, such as groceries, entertainment, and travel expenses.

To create a budget, start by listing all of your expected sources of income for the period you are budgeting for. This might include your salary or wages, as well as any additional sources of income such as rental income or investment dividends. Next, list all of your fixed and variable expenses, including any debt payments you need to make.

Once you have listed all of your income and expenses, subtract your total expenses from your total income to get your net income. If your expenses are higher than your income, you will need to make some adjustments to your budget in order to reduce your expenses or increase your income. This might involve cutting back on non-essential expenses or finding ways to increase your income, such as taking on a side job or freelance work.

It's important to regularly review and adjust your budget as needed, particularly if you experience any major changes in your income or expenses. By staying on top of your budget, you can ensure that you are making the most of your financial resources and staying on track to achieve your long-term financial goals.

## Importance of budgeting

Budgeting is an essential aspect of financial management, especially for businesses that want to grow without overspending. It helps to set realistic financial goals, track income and expenses, and make informed financial decisions. Budgeting helps businesses to prioritize expenses, reduce unnecessary spending, and ensure that available resources are used efficiently.

Without a budget, businesses may struggle to manage their finances effectively, leading to cash flow problems, overspending, and even bankruptcy. Budgeting also provides a framework for monitoring financial progress and making necessary adjustments along the way.

Creating and following a budget can be a challenging process, especially for businesses that are not used to budgeting. However, it is an essential component of growing a business on a budget and ensuring long-term financial stability.

Creating a realistic budget plan is crucial for the success of any business. A budget plan helps to establish clear financial goals and priorities and provides a roadmap for achieving them. It is important to create a budget plan that is realistic and achievable, taking into account all the different expenses and income sources of the business.

To create a realistic budget plan, start by identifying all the sources of income for your business. This may include sales revenue, investments, and any other sources of income. Next, list out all the expenses, including fixed expenses like rent, salaries, and utilities, as well as variable expenses like advertising, marketing, and supplies. Make sure to include any anticipated expenses that may arise in the future, such as repairs or upgrades to equipment.

Once you have a clear understanding of your income and expenses, you can begin to allocate your resources accordingly. Identify areas where you can cut costs or reduce expenses, and consider how you can increase revenue through new products or services, or by expanding into new markets. When creating your budget plan, be sure to set realistic goals and timelines, and factor in any unexpected expenses or changes in your business environment.

It's important to monitor your budget plan regularly and make adjustments as necessary. Review your budget plan on a monthly or quarterly basis to ensure that you're on track to meet your financial goals. By creating a realistic budget plan and sticking to it, you can help your business stay financially stable and achieve long-term success.

## Strategies for reducing expenses

Reducing expenses is a critical aspect of creating a budget plan for growing a business without breaking the bank. Here are some strategies to help reduce expenses:

1. Review and renegotiate contracts: Analyze your current contracts with vendors, suppliers, and service providers to identify opportunities for negotiation. Look for lower rates or alternative service providers that can offer similar services at a lower cost.

2. Cut unnecessary expenses: Examine your expenses to determine which ones are essential and which ones are not. Eliminate expenses that are not crucial to your business operations.

3. Go paperless: By going paperless, you can save money on printing and mailing costs. Switch to electronic billing and invoicing, and encourage customers to pay electronically.

4. Implement energy-saving measures: Energy-saving measures such as turning off lights and equipment when not in use, using energy-efficient light bulbs, and upgrading to energy-efficient equipment can help reduce your utility bills.

5. Use open-source software: Open-source software can be a cost-effective alternative to proprietary software. Look for open-source software that can replace the costly software you are currently using.

6. Outsource non-core functions: Outsourcing non-core functions such as accounting, payroll, and IT support can be a cost-effective way to reduce expenses.

7. Encourage telecommuting: Allowing employees to work from home can save money on office space and utilities.

By implementing these strategies, you can reduce your expenses and create a more realistic budget plan for your business.

There are several strategies that can be implemented to reduce expenses and stay within your budget. One effective approach is to negotiate with vendors to lower prices or to find alternative suppliers that offer better rates. This can involve exploring different options for raw materials, equipment, or services to find the most cost-effective solutions.

Another approach is to optimize your inventory management to reduce waste and minimize carrying costs. This can involve implementing just-in-time (JIT) inventory systems, reducing excess inventory, and improving forecasting accuracy to ensure you have the right amount of inventory on hand.

You can also consider reducing unnecessary expenses such as unnecessary subscriptions, travel expenses, or other discretionary spending. This requires a careful review of all business expenses to identify areas where costs can be cut without negatively impacting operations.

In addition, it is important to prioritize expenses based on their impact on revenue generation and profitability. This means focusing on investments that have a direct impact on the bottom line, such as marketing and sales initiatives, while reducing or eliminating expenses that do not contribute significantly to revenue or profitability.

By implementing these strategies, businesses can significantly reduce their expenses and create a more sustainable financial position. However, it is important to strike a balance between cost-cutting and investment in key growth areas to ensure long-term success.

# CHAPTER IV

## Marketing on a Budget

Marketing is a critical aspect of growing any business, and it can be costly. However, there are several low-cost marketing strategies that entrepreneurs can implement to promote their brand and increase their customer base without breaking the bank. This chapter will discuss the importance of marketing and highlight low-cost strategies that entrepreneurs can utilize to promote their business on a budget.

**Understanding the Importance of Marketing**

Marketing is a critical aspect of any business, as it helps to create brand awareness and attract new customers. However, many entrepreneurs fail to recognize the importance of marketing or allocate sufficient funds to their marketing budget. This can have significant negative impacts on their business's growth potential.

Entrepreneurs should understand that marketing is not a one-time activity, and it requires continuous efforts to maintain brand visibility and attract new customers. Therefore, it is essential to incorporate marketing into your overall business plan and allocate sufficient funds to your marketing budget.

**Low-Cost Marketing Strategies**

1.  Content Marketing: Content marketing involves creating and distributing valuable, relevant, and consistent content to attract and retain a clearly defined audience. This can include blog posts, social media content, videos, and infographics. Content marketing is an effective way to build brand awareness and attract new customers without incurring significant costs.

2.  Referral Marketing: Referral marketing involves encouraging your existing customers to refer new customers to your business. You can offer incentives to your customers for each new customer they refer to your business, such as discounts or free products. This strategy is cost-effective and can help you attract new customers while also rewarding your existing customers.

3.  Social Media Marketing: Social media platforms such as Facebook, Twitter, and Instagram provide a low-cost way to promote

your business and connect with your customers. You can use these platforms to share your content, engage with your followers, and run targeted advertising campaigns to attract new customers.

4. Email Marketing: Email marketing is a cost-effective way to reach out to your existing customers and promote your business. You can use email marketing to share news and updates, promote new products or services, and offer exclusive discounts or promotions.

## Leveraging Social Media and Other Digital Platforms

In addition to the low-cost marketing strategies outlined above, entrepreneurs can also leverage social media and other digital platforms to promote their business. These platforms provide a cost-effective way to reach a broader audience and increase brand awareness.

Entrepreneurs should focus on building a strong online presence by creating and maintaining a website, social media profiles, and other digital assets. They should also ensure that their online presence is consistent with their brand and messaging.

Marketing is a critical aspect of growing any business, but it can be costly. However, entrepreneurs can implement several low-cost marketing strategies to promote their business and attract new customers without breaking the bank. Content marketing, referral marketing, social media marketing, and email marketing are all cost-effective strategies that entrepreneurs can utilize to promote their business on a budget. By leveraging social media and other digital platforms, entrepreneurs can increase their brand awareness and attract a broader audience while maintaining financial stability.

## Understanding the importance of marketing

Marketing is a critical component of any business, regardless of its size or industry. It is the process of promoting and selling products or services to potential customers with the aim of generating revenue and building a strong customer base. Effective marketing can help businesses increase their visibility, build brand awareness, and ultimately boost sales and revenue.

Marketing on a budget is particularly important for small businesses that may not have a lot of resources to devote to advertising and promotion. By understanding the importance of marketing, business owners can allocate their limited resources in a way that maximizes their impact.

Marketing helps businesses to:

- Build brand awareness: Through marketing efforts, businesses can create a distinct brand identity that resonates with their target audience. This can include creating a unique logo, slogan, and marketing message that sets them apart from competitors.

- Reach new customers: Marketing efforts can help businesses reach new customers who may not have been aware of their products or services previously. This can include leveraging social media, email marketing, and other digital channels to connect with potential customers.

- Increase sales and revenue: Effective marketing can lead to increased sales and revenue by driving more traffic to a business's website, generating more leads, and converting more prospects into paying customers.

In short, marketing is essential for businesses that want to grow and succeed. By developing a strong marketing strategy, businesses can reach new customers, build brand awareness, and increase sales and revenue.

Marketing is a critical aspect of any business. It involves creating awareness about your products or services and convincing potential customers to buy from you. Without marketing, even the best products may remain unsold. It is, therefore, essential to understand the importance of marketing when growing a business on a budget. By having a clear understanding of what marketing is and its importance, business owners can develop effective marketing strategies that are both cost-effective and efficient.

Marketing can help businesses to differentiate themselves from their competitors. By creating a unique brand identity and communicating it to potential customers, businesses can stand out in a crowded marketplace. Effective marketing can also help to establish trust and credibility with customers, making it easier to generate repeat business and referrals.

Furthermore, marketing helps businesses to target the right audience. By identifying the specific needs and preferences of their target market, businesses can tailor their marketing messages and reach their ideal customers. This can lead to higher conversion rates, increased sales, and ultimately, more revenue.

In summary, marketing is critical to the success of any business, and understanding its importance is crucial when growing a business on a budget. By developing effective marketing strategies, businesses can achieve their growth goals while minimizing costs.

## Low-cost marketing strategies

Low-cost marketing strategies are essential for small businesses that are growing on a budget. Here are some effective low-cost marketing strategies that businesses can use:

1. Social media marketing: Social media platforms such as Facebook, Instagram, Twitter, and LinkedIn are excellent tools for businesses to reach out to their target audience. Social media marketing is cost-effective and allows businesses to reach a large audience at a low cost.

2. Content marketing: Creating informative and engaging content that provides value to the target audience is an effective marketing strategy. Businesses can use blog posts, infographics, videos, and other types of content to attract and engage their audience.

3. Email marketing: Email marketing is an affordable way to reach out to customers and prospects. Businesses can use email to share company news, promotions, and updates, and build relationships with their audience.

4. Referral marketing: Referral marketing is a powerful way to grow a business. Encouraging satisfied customers to refer their friends and family to the business is an effective way to increase sales at little to no cost.

5. Networking: Attending industry events, conferences, and trade shows is an excellent way to meet potential customers and partners. Networking provides opportunities to build relationships and promote the business to a wider audience.

6. Guerrilla Marketing: Guerrilla marketing involves using unconventional marketing

tactics to promote a business. Examples include graffiti marketing, flash mobs, and street performances.

By leveraging these low-cost marketing strategies, businesses can effectively reach their target audience, build brand awareness, and drive sales while staying within their budget.

## Leveraging social media and other digital platforms

Social media and digital platforms have become integral parts of marketing in the modern business world. They offer an affordable and effective way for businesses to reach a large audience and engage with potential customers.

One of the most popular social media platforms for businesses is Facebook. A business can create a Facebook page and use it to share information about their products or services, engage with customers, and run targeted advertising campaigns. Instagram and Twitter are also popular platforms for businesses, especially those targeting younger audiences.

Another effective way to market on a budget is through email marketing. Businesses can create an email list of customers and potential customers who have opted in to receive emails from the company. Emails can be used to share promotions, new product launches, and other important information.

In addition to social media and email marketing, businesses can also leverage other digital platforms such as Google My Business, Yelp, and other online directories. These platforms allow businesses to provide accurate and detailed information about their business, including contact information, business hours, reviews, and more.

Overall, digital marketing offers a cost-effective way for businesses to reach a large audience and build their brand. By leveraging social media and other digital platforms, businesses can create a strong online presence and drive more traffic to their website, ultimately leading to more sales and revenue.

There are many social media and digital platforms available that can be leveraged to promote a business without breaking the bank. Here are some low-cost strategies for using social media and digital platforms:

1. Create and optimize social media profiles: Start by creating profiles on the most relevant social media platforms for your business, such as Facebook, Instagram, Twitter, LinkedIn, and

Pinterest. Ensure that your profiles are complete, include a professional profile picture and cover photo, and include all the necessary information about your business, such as the website, hours of operation, and contact information.

2. Share valuable content: Share relevant and valuable content on your social media platforms to attract and engage with your audience. This can include blog posts, infographics, videos, and images. Make sure the content you share is related to your business and is of interest to your target audience.

3. Engage with your followers: Respond to comments and messages on your social media platforms promptly. This shows your followers that you value their engagement and care about their opinions.

4. Run social media ads: Running targeted social media ads can be a cost-effective way to reach a larger audience. You can target specific demographics, interests, and behaviors to

ensure that your ads reach the most relevant audience.

5. Utilize email marketing: Email marketing is a great way to reach out to your existing customers and promote your products or services. You can send newsletters, promotions, and other updates to keep your customers engaged and informed.

6. Collaborate with influencers: Influencer marketing involves partnering with social media influencers who have a large following to promote your products or services. This can be a great way to reach a new audience and gain credibility in your industry.

By leveraging social media and digital platforms, businesses can effectively promote their products and services without breaking the bank.

# CHAPTER V

## Maximizing Efficiency

One of the biggest challenges of growing a business on a budget is finding ways to do more with less. Maximizing efficiency is critical for businesses that want to grow without overspending. This chapter will explore various strategies for streamlining operations, implementing technology, and outsourcing to increase efficiency and reduce costs.

**Streamlining Operations**

Streamlining operations involves identifying and eliminating inefficiencies in business processes. This can help reduce costs and improve overall productivity. Some strategies for streamlining operations include:

1. Automating repetitive tasks: Businesses can use software to automate repetitive tasks such as data entry, invoicing, and payroll processing. This can save time and reduce errors.

2. Simplifying processes: Simplifying processes can help reduce the time and resources required to complete tasks. This can involve

reorganizing workflows or simplifying product lines.

3. Standardizing procedures: Standardizing procedures can help improve consistency and reduce errors. This can involve creating standard operating procedures (SOPs) for tasks such as customer service or order processing.

**Implementing Technology**

Implementing technology can help businesses improve efficiency and reduce costs. Some strategies for implementing technology include:

1. Using cloud-based software: Cloud-based software allows businesses to access software and data from anywhere with an internet connection. This can save businesses money on hardware and software costs and increase productivity.

2. Adopting collaboration tools: Collaboration tools such as project management software and video conferencing can help improve communication and productivity.

3. Using data analytics: Data analytics can help businesses make more informed decisions by

providing insights into customer behavior, sales trends, and other key metrics.

## Outsourcing vs. Hiring In-House

Outsourcing can be a cost-effective way to increase efficiency and reduce costs. Some tasks that can be outsourced include bookkeeping, customer service, and social media management. However, outsourcing also has some drawbacks, including loss of control and communication challenges.

Alternatively, hiring in-house can provide businesses with more control over the quality of work and better communication with employees. However, this can be more expensive and time-consuming than outsourcing.

By maximizing efficiency, businesses can reduce costs and increase productivity, enabling them to grow on a budget.

### Streamlining operations to reduce costs

Streamlining operations is an effective way to reduce costs and increase efficiency. When a business operates inefficiently, it can result in wasted time and resources, which can ultimately impact the bottom line. By streamlining operations, a business can reduce waste and increase productivity, leading to cost savings.

One way to streamline operations is to identify and eliminate any unnecessary steps in a process. This could involve reorganizing the way work is done, automating certain tasks, or reducing the number of people involved in a process. For example, a business might find that by automating the ordering process for supplies, they can reduce the time and resources needed to manage inventory.

Another way to streamline operations is to implement systems and processes that enable better communication and collaboration. This could involve using project management tools to assign tasks and track progress, or setting up regular team meetings to ensure everyone is on the same page.

It's important to regularly review and analyze processes to identify areas for improvement. By monitoring key performance indicators (KPIs) and soliciting feedback from employees, a business can identify areas where processes can be optimized or streamlined.

Overall, streamlining operations is an essential part of maximizing efficiency and reducing costs. By eliminating waste and improving productivity, a business can operate more effectively and achieve greater success.

One way to streamline operations and reduce costs is by optimizing your supply chain management. This means evaluating your current suppliers, negotiating better prices, and exploring new suppliers to get the best deals on the materials or products you need.

Another strategy is to implement lean manufacturing techniques, which focus on reducing waste and increasing efficiency. This involves identifying and eliminating any unnecessary steps or processes in your production line.

You can also consider outsourcing certain tasks to third-party providers who specialize in those areas. For example, you may outsource your accounting or IT services instead of hiring in-house staff, which can save you money on salaries and benefits.

Finally, implementing technology can help you automate certain tasks, which can save time and reduce errors. For example, you may invest in inventory management software to help you track your inventory levels and minimize overstocking or stockouts.

By maximizing efficiency, you can reduce your operating costs and improve your bottom line, without sacrificing quality or customer satisfaction.

## Implementing technology to increase efficiency

Implementing technology can help increase efficiency and reduce costs for businesses. By automating certain tasks and using software tools to streamline operations, businesses can save time and money. For example, accounting software can help manage finances and create financial reports, reducing the need for manual data entry and saving time. Customer relationship management (CRM) software can help businesses manage customer interactions and track sales leads.

Other examples of technology that can increase efficiency include project management tools, scheduling software, and online communication platforms. By using these tools, businesses can better manage their workflow and improve communication between team members.

It's important to carefully evaluate different technology options and choose the ones that will have the greatest impact on efficiency and cost reduction. Businesses should also invest in employee training to ensure that everyone is comfortable using the new tools and maximizing their potential.

Implementing technology to increase efficiency can significantly improve business operations and reduce costs. For example, implementing a customer relationship management (CRM) system can help automate tasks such as lead generation, customer management, and sales tracking. This can help reduce the need for manual labor and increase productivity.

Another example is implementing inventory management software, which can help businesses keep track of their stock levels, reduce wastage and prevent stockouts. This can help businesses avoid the costs associated with overstocking or understocking their inventory.

Moreover, cloud-based technologies can help businesses reduce costs associated with hardware, maintenance, and IT staff. Cloud-based solutions offer flexibility and scalability, and businesses can choose to pay for only what they need, making it a cost-effective option for small businesses.

Overall, implementing technology can help businesses streamline their operations, reduce costs, and increase efficiency.

Outsourcing vs. hiring in-house is a critical decision that businesses need to make to maximize efficiency while keeping costs low. In-house hiring can provide more control over business operations and offer better communication between team members. However, it can also be more expensive due to additional costs such as employee benefits, salaries, and taxes. Outsourcing, on the other hand, can be more cost-effective as it allows businesses to hire specialized teams to perform specific tasks or projects without the added expense of employee benefits and salaries.

Outsourcing can also provide access to a broader pool of talent and expertise that may not be available in-house. However, it can be challenging to manage outsourced teams and ensure that they deliver quality work within the desired timeline. Therefore, it's essential to evaluate the pros and cons of each option carefully and choose the one that aligns with the business's goals and budget.

One approach is to outsource non-core functions while keeping critical operations in-house. For example, a business may choose to outsource its bookkeeping or social media management while keeping its product development and customer service functions in-house.

Ultimately, the decision to outsource or hire in-house depends on the business's unique circumstances, goals, and budget. A thorough evaluation of the available options can help businesses determine the best approach to maximize efficiency while keeping costs low.

Outsourcing certain tasks can be a cost-effective way to increase efficiency while keeping costs down. For example, outsourcing tasks such as bookkeeping, social media management, and customer service can free up time and resources for the business to focus on core competencies. It can also reduce the need for additional office space, equipment, and other overhead costs associated with hiring in-house.

However, outsourcing also comes with its own set of challenges. It can be difficult to find reliable and trustworthy vendors, and communication and cultural differences can create additional hurdles. It's important to weigh the pros and cons of outsourcing vs. hiring in-house based on the specific needs and circumstances of the business.

When it comes to hiring in-house, it's important to carefully consider the true cost of hiring and retaining employees, including salary, benefits, taxes, and other overhead costs. Hiring the right employees can be a significant investment, but it can also bring valuable expertise and skills to the business.

Overall, finding the right balance between outsourcing and hiring in-house can help a business maximize efficiency while keeping costs under control.

# CHAPTER VI
## Financing and Funding Options

Financing and funding are crucial aspects of growing a business. Without proper funding, it can be difficult for businesses to expand and achieve their goals. In this chapter, we'll explore different financing and funding options available to small businesses.

1. Identifying financing options There are several financing options available to small businesses, including:

- Small Business Administration (SBA) loans

- Traditional bank loans

- Microloans

- Crowdfunding

- Angel investors

- Venture capital

2. Pros and cons of different funding sources Each funding source has its own advantages and disadvantages. It's important to weigh the pros and cons of each option before making a decision. For example, SBA loans may have

lower interest rates, but they can be difficult to obtain. On the other hand, crowdfunding may be easier to access, but it may not provide as much funding as other sources.

3. Preparing a strong funding application Regardless of which funding source you choose, it's important to prepare a strong funding application. This includes developing a detailed business plan, providing accurate financial statements, and highlighting the potential for growth and profitability.

4. Managing debt When obtaining financing, it's important to manage debt properly. This includes making timely payments and avoiding taking on too much debt, which can strain your business's finances.

5. Balancing equity and control When accepting funding from investors, it's important to balance equity and control. Investors may want to have a say in how the business is run, but it's important to maintain control over key decisions.

By understanding the different financing and funding options available, small business owners can make informed decisions about how to grow their businesses while maintaining financial stability.

Another financing option is through venture capitalists (VCs) or angel investors. VCs and angel investors are individuals or firms that provide capital to businesses in exchange for ownership equity or convertible debt. Unlike traditional loans, these investors are willing to take on more risk and typically invest in businesses that have the potential for high growth and returns.

While securing financing from VCs or angel investors can be a great option for businesses with high growth potential, it is important to carefully consider the terms of the investment and the potential impact on ownership and decision-making in the company. It is also crucial to have a well-prepared pitch and business plan to present to potential investors.

Another funding option to consider is crowdfunding, which involves raising capital through a large number of small contributions from individuals, typically through online platforms. Crowdfunding can be a great way to generate buzz and interest around a product or service while also securing the necessary funding. However, it requires a significant amount of effort to create and promote a compelling crowdfunding campaign.

Finally, some businesses may qualify for government-backed loans or grants, which can provide low-interest financing or funding that does not need to be repaid. These options can be especially beneficial for small businesses that may have difficulty securing financing from traditional sources.

It is important to carefully evaluate all financing and funding options and determine which options are the best fit for your business based on your specific needs and goals.

## Identifying financing options

Identifying financing options is an important step for any business that wants to grow without breaking the bank. There are many financing options available to businesses, and choosing the right one can make a significant difference in terms of cost and impact on the business.

One common financing option for businesses is a traditional bank loan. This type of loan typically requires a good credit history and collateral to secure the loan. Another option is a line of credit, which can be used as needed and typically requires a good credit score. Businesses can also look into alternative financing options such as crowdfunding, angel investors, venture capital, or grants.

When identifying financing options, it is important for businesses to evaluate the interest rates, repayment terms, and any associated fees or costs. It is also important to consider the potential impact on the business, such as the level of control given to investors or the impact on cash flow.

Ultimately, choosing the right financing option depends on the specific needs and goals of the business. It is important to carefully consider all available options and to work with a financial advisor or accountant to make an informed decision.

In addition to traditional loans and lines of credit, there are several other financing options available for small businesses. These include:

1. Crowdfunding: Crowdfunding platforms like Kickstarter and Indiegogo allow businesses to raise money from a large group of people by offering incentives or rewards in exchange for their financial support.

2. Grants: There are many government and private organizations that offer grants to small businesses. These grants can be used to fund specific projects or initiatives.

3. Angel investors: Angel investors are individuals who provide funding for small businesses in exchange for equity in the company.

4. Venture capital: Venture capital firms provide funding to businesses that have high growth potential in exchange for equity in the company.

5. Factoring: Factoring is a financing option that allows businesses to sell their outstanding invoices to a third party at a discount in exchange for immediate cash.

It is important to carefully consider the terms and conditions of each financing option and to choose the option that is best suited to the needs of your business.

When it comes to financing a business, there are several funding sources available. Each of these funding sources has its own set of pros and cons that business owners should consider before making a decision.

1. Self-Funding: This involves using personal savings or assets to fund the business. The pros of self-funding include retaining full control of the business and not having to pay interest on loans. However, it can be risky, and business owners may not have enough capital to fully finance their business.

2. Friends and Family: Borrowing money from friends and family can be a good option for some entrepreneurs, as it can be easier to obtain than other funding sources. However, mixing business with personal relationships can be risky and may cause tension.

3. Bank Loans: Traditional bank loans can provide a large amount of capital, but they can be difficult to obtain, especially for small businesses. Bank loans typically require

collateral, and the approval process can take a long time.

4. Small Business Administration (SBA) Loans: SBA loans are government-backed loans that are designed to help small businesses. They can be easier to obtain than traditional bank loans, and they often have lower interest rates.

5. Crowdfunding: Crowdfunding involves raising money from a large number of people through an online platform. This can be a good option for businesses that have a large following or a unique product, but it can also be challenging to stand out from the crowd.

6. Angel Investors: Angel investors are individuals who provide funding for startups in exchange for equity. They can provide a large amount of capital and often have experience in the industry, but they may also expect a large return on their investment.

7. Venture Capital: Venture capital firms provide funding for startups in exchange for equity. They can provide a large amount of capital and often have experience in the industry, but they may also expect a large return on their

investment and may want to have a say in the management of the business.

It is important to carefully consider the pros and cons of each funding source before making a decision. Business owners should also consider their long-term goals and how the funding will impact their business in the future.

When considering funding sources, it's important to weigh the pros and cons of each option. For example, taking out a loan can provide a lump sum of cash to use for business expenses, but it also comes with interest and repayment requirements. Similarly, seeking out investors can bring in valuable funding and resources, but it also means giving up a share of ownership and control over the business.

Other funding options may include crowdfunding, grants, and government loans or programs. Each option comes with its own set of benefits and drawbacks, and it's important for business owners to research and evaluate which options may be the best fit for their specific needs and goals.

Additionally, preparing a strong funding application is crucial to securing funding. This may involve developing a detailed business plan, preparing financial projections and reports, and demonstrating a strong understanding of the market and industry. Seeking advice and guidance from financial professionals or consultants can also be helpful in navigating the complex world of business financing.

Pros and cons of each of the funding options mentioned:

1. Crowdfunding: Crowdfunding platforms like Kickstarter and Indiegogo allow businesses to raise money from a large number of people. Pros include low barrier to entry, minimal financial risk, and potential for viral exposure. However, the success rate is low, and there's no guarantee that the funding goal will be met.

2. Grants: Grants are free money that don't have to be repaid. Pros include not having to give up equity or ownership, and the possibility of receiving funding for research and development. However, the application process is often competitive, and there are usually restrictions on how the money can be used.

3. Government loans: Government loans are typically offered at lower interest rates and longer repayment terms than private loans.

Pros include relatively low-interest rates and flexible repayment terms. However, government loans are often harder to qualify for, and the application process can be lengthy.

4.  Venture capital: Venture capital firms invest in high-growth startups in exchange for equity. Pros include access to large amounts of funding, business expertise, and mentorship. However, venture capital firms often demand a large ownership stake and may require a say in business decisions.

5.  Angel investors: Angel investors are wealthy individuals who invest in startups in exchange for equity. Pros include access to funding, business expertise, and mentorship. However, angel investors also typically demand a large ownership stake and may require a say in business decisions.

6.  Bank Loans: Bank loans are a traditional source of funding and can be a good option for established businesses with a solid credit history. Pros include lower interest rates and predictable repayment terms. However, the

application process can be stringent, and collateral may be required.

7. Small Business Administration Loans: SBA loans are offered by the government and are designed to help small businesses. Pros include low-interest rates and long repayment terms. However, the application process can be lengthy and may require a lot of documentation.

8. Friends and family: Borrowing from friends and family can be a quick and easy way to get funding. Pros include flexible repayment terms and a willingness to help out. However, mixing business with personal relationships can be risky, and defaulting on the loan can cause strain in the relationship.

9. Self-funding: Self-funding involves using personal savings or assets to finance the business. Pros include complete control over the business and no need to pay back investors. However, self-funding can be risky, and it can be difficult to generate enough capital to grow the business.

Preparing a strong funding application is crucial to securing funding from investors, lenders, or grant-giving organizations. A strong application can help demonstrate the potential of your business and persuade investors that your business is worth their investment.

Here are some tips to prepare a strong funding application:

1. Know the requirements: Before applying for funding, it's essential to know the specific requirements of the funding source. Make sure you understand the eligibility criteria, application deadlines, required documentation, and funding amount available.

2. Craft a compelling pitch: You must be able to articulate your business idea and why it's worth funding. Your pitch should highlight your unique selling proposition, target market, growth potential, and competitive advantage.

3. Prepare a detailed business plan: Your business plan should outline your company's goals, objectives, and strategies for achieving them. It

should also include financial projections, market research, and management team bios.

4. Include a strong financial statement: Your financial statement should include accurate financial projections, cash flow analysis, and balance sheets. It's essential to provide realistic projections based on industry benchmarks and your business's unique situation.

5. Highlight your team's qualifications: Investors want to know that your team has the experience and skills needed to execute your business plan successfully. Highlight your team's qualifications, expertise, and accomplishments.

6. Be transparent: Be honest and transparent about your business's strengths and weaknesses. Investors appreciate transparency and want to know that you're aware of the risks and challenges facing your business.

By following these tips, you can increase your chances of securing funding and growing your business.

To prepare a strong funding application, it is important to have a clear business plan that outlines the company's goals, financial projections, and growth strategy. The application should also clearly articulate how the funds will be used and the potential return on investment for the funder.

In addition, it is important to research the specific requirements and expectations of the funding source, whether it is a crowdfunding platform, grant program, or venture capital firm. Each funding source will have different criteria and application processes, so it is important to tailor the application to meet those specific requirements.

It is also important to have a strong pitch that clearly communicates the value proposition of the business and why it is a good investment opportunity. This can involve highlighting the unique aspects of the business, the potential market size, and the competitive landscape.

Overall, preparing a strong funding application requires careful planning, research, and attention to detail. By following best practices and tailoring the application to the specific funding source, businesses can increase their chances of securing the necessary funds to grow and scale their operations.

Chapter VII of the book focuses on the strategies for scaling and growing your business while maintaining financial stability. It emphasizes the importance of having a clear plan for growth and being prepared for the challenges that come with it.

The chapter starts by discussing the need to prepare for growth by evaluating the current state of the business and identifying potential areas for expansion. It emphasizes the importance of having a solid business plan and being aware of market trends and competition.

The next section discusses strategies for scaling your business while maintaining financial stability. It emphasizes the need for careful financial planning and management to avoid overspending and accumulating debt. The chapter also provides tips on how to control costs and maximize revenue through effective pricing strategies, operational efficiency, and customer retention.

The chapter then highlights common mistakes that businesses make when scaling, such as expanding too quickly, overestimating revenue, and neglecting cash flow management. It emphasizes the importance of learning from these mistakes and adapting strategies accordingly.

The final section discusses the role of leadership in scaling and growth. It emphasizes the importance of building a strong team, delegating responsibilities, and creating a culture of innovation and continuous improvement. It also provides advice on how to stay motivated and focused during the growth process.

Overall, Chapter VII provides valuable insights and practical strategies for businesses looking to scale and grow while maintaining financial stability.

## Preparing for growth

Preparing for growth is a critical step for any business looking to scale. It requires careful planning and execution to ensure that the growth process is smooth and sustainable. Below are some key steps businesses can take to prepare for growth:

1. Develop a Growth Strategy: Before embarking on any growth initiative, businesses need to have a clear growth strategy in place. This strategy should outline the specific growth

goals, the resources required, and the steps to be taken to achieve those goals.

2. Invest in Infrastructure: As businesses grow, their infrastructure needs will also grow. It is essential to invest in infrastructure such as technology, equipment, and personnel to support the growth.

3. Improve Operations: Inefficient operations can hinder growth, so businesses need to streamline and improve their processes. This can involve outsourcing certain tasks or investing in automation to increase efficiency.

4. Expand the Customer Base: To achieve sustainable growth, businesses must expand their customer base. This can be done through marketing initiatives, improving customer service, and developing new products or services.

5. Hire the Right People: As businesses grow, they will need to hire new employees to support their expansion. It is important to hire the right people who are aligned with the company's values and culture and have the necessary skills to help the business grow.

6. Manage Finances: As businesses grow, their financial needs will also change. It is essential to manage finances carefully and invest in the areas that will support growth while also minimizing risks.

7. Monitor Progress: It is important to monitor the progress of growth initiatives regularly. This will enable businesses to make adjustments as needed and stay on track towards their growth goals.

To prepare for growth, businesses need to consider their current market position, target audience, and competition. They should assess their existing resources and determine what additional resources they will need to scale up their operations.

It is also essential to establish clear goals and objectives for growth, as well as a plan to achieve them. This plan should include a timeline, a budget, and strategies for marketing, sales, and operational expansion.

Another critical factor in preparing for growth is building a strong team. Business owners should identify the key roles they need to fill and recruit talented individuals who can help drive growth and take the business to the next level.

Finally, businesses should continuously evaluate and adjust their growth plans based on their progress and changes in the market. It is essential to remain agile and adaptable to stay ahead of the competition and ensure long-term success.

By following these steps, businesses can effectively prepare for growth and set themselves up for long-term success.

## Strategies for scaling your business while maintaining financial stability

Scaling a business requires a delicate balance between growth and financial stability. Here are some strategies that can help you scale your business while maintaining financial stability:

1. Prioritize profitable growth: When scaling your business, it's important to focus on profitable growth. This means prioritizing revenue streams and customer segments that are most profitable for your business. It's also important to carefully manage expenses and investments to ensure they align with your growth strategy.

2. Invest in your team: As your business grows, it's important to invest in your team to ensure they have the skills and resources they need to support your growth. This may include providing training and development opportunities, offering competitive compensation and benefits packages, and creating a positive work environment.

3. Leverage technology: Technology can help you scale your business more efficiently and effectively. Consider implementing tools and systems that can automate processes, improve productivity, and enhance customer experience. However, be cautious of overspending on unnecessary technology that may not provide a return on investment.

4. Diversify your revenue streams: Diversifying your revenue streams can help mitigate risk and create more stability as your business grows. This may include expanding your product or service offerings, entering new markets, or developing strategic partnerships.

5. Monitor and measure performance: It's important to regularly monitor and measure

your business performance to ensure you're on track to achieving your growth goals while maintaining financial stability. This may include tracking key performance indicators, conducting regular financial analyses, and adjusting your strategy as needed.

6. Manage cash flow: As your business grows, cash flow management becomes even more critical. Make sure you have a clear understanding of your cash flow projections and take proactive steps to manage your cash flow, such as optimizing your payment terms, reducing expenses, and managing inventory levels.

7. Strategic partnerships: By partnering with other businesses, you can access new markets, increase production capacity, and reduce costs through shared resources.

8. Automation: Automating certain tasks and processes can increase efficiency and reduce costs.

9. Outsourcing: Outsourcing non-core functions can free up time and resources to focus on core business activities.

10. Implementing systems and processes: Standardizing your business processes can help ensure consistency and efficiency as you scale.

11. Hiring strategically: Hiring the right people at the right time can help you scale while maintaining financial stability. Consider hiring freelancers or contractors before committing to full-time employees.

Overall, scaling a business requires careful planning, disciplined execution, and ongoing evaluation and adjustment. By implementing these strategies, you can position your business for sustainable growth and financial stability.

By implementing these strategies, you can scale your business while maintaining financial stability and avoid common pitfalls that can lead to financial instability.

## Avoiding common mistakes

Scaling a business can be challenging, and there are common mistakes that entrepreneurs make during the process. Here are some mistakes to avoid:

1. Scaling too quickly: Rapid growth may seem appealing, but it can put a strain on your

resources and infrastructure. Make sure you have a solid plan in place and the necessary resources to handle increased demand before scaling.

2. Neglecting cash flow: Cash flow is critical to the success of any business, and scaling can put a strain on your finances. Make sure you have a solid understanding of your cash flow and have strategies in place to maintain it.

3. Not investing in the right areas: It's important to invest in areas that will help your business grow and succeed. Make sure you prioritize investments in areas that will have the greatest impact on your business.

4. Failing to adapt: As your business grows, you'll need to adapt to changing market conditions and customer needs. Failing to adapt can result in missed opportunities and lost revenue.

5. Overextending yourself: Scaling can be expensive, and it's important not to overextend yourself financially. Make sure you have a solid understanding of your finances and the costs associated with scaling your business.

By avoiding these common mistakes and planning for growth, you can successfully scale your business while maintaining financial stability.

# CHAPTER VIII
## Managing Your Business Finances

Managing your business finances is an essential part of running a successful business. Proper financial management can help you make informed decisions, stay on track with your budget, and avoid financial pitfalls that could threaten the stability of your business. In this chapter, we will discuss some important tips for managing your business finances effectively.

1. Keep Accurate Records

Keeping accurate financial records is essential to managing your business finances effectively. You should keep track of all financial transactions, including income and expenses, on a regular basis. This will help you identify any cash flow issues early on and ensure that you are staying within your budget.

2. Create a Budget

Creating a budget is an important step in managing your business finances. Your budget should include all of your anticipated expenses, such as rent, utilities, payroll, and inventory, as well as your anticipated income. By creating a budget, you can ensure that you are allocating your resources effectively and staying on track with your financial goals.

3.  Monitor Your Cash Flow

Monitoring your cash flow is another important part of managing your business finances. You should keep track of your cash inflows and outflows on a regular basis, and use this information to identify any potential cash flow issues. By monitoring your cash flow, you can make informed decisions about when to make investments or cut back on expenses.

4.  Manage Your Debt

Managing your debt is another important aspect of managing your business finances. You should keep track of all of your outstanding debts, including loans and credit card balances, and make sure that you are making your payments on time. If you are struggling with debt, you may need to consider debt consolidation or other debt management strategies.

5.  Plan for Taxes

Planning for taxes is an important part of managing your business finances. You should keep track of all of your business expenses and income throughout the year, and use this information to prepare for tax season. You may also want to work with a tax professional to ensure that you are taking advantage of all available tax deductions and credits.

6.  Invest in Accounting Software

Investing in accounting software can help you manage your business finances more efficiently. Accounting software can help you keep track of your financial transactions, create invoices and financial reports, and stay on top of your tax obligations. There are many accounting software options available, so be sure to do your research to find the right one for your business.

7.  Work with a Financial Advisor

Working with a financial advisor can also be a helpful strategy for managing your business finances. A financial advisor can help you create a comprehensive financial plan, identify potential financial risks, and provide guidance on how to manage your investments and debt.

In conclusion, managing your business finances is an essential part of running a successful business. By keeping accurate records, creating a budget, monitoring your cash flow, managing your debt, planning for taxes, investing in accounting software, and working with a financial advisor, you can ensure that you are managing your business finances effectively and staying on track with your financial goals.

## Developing a budget

Developing a budget is an essential part of managing your business finances. It is important to have a clear understanding of your business's financial situation, which can be achieved through regular monitoring and forecasting of your revenues, expenses, and cash flow. A budget serves as a financial roadmap, helping you make informed decisions and prioritize spending based on your business's needs and goals.

To develop a budget, follow these steps:

1. Gather financial information: Collect all financial information relevant to your business, including revenue and expense reports, bank statements, and tax returns.

2. Determine your revenue sources: Identify all revenue sources, such as sales, services, and

investments. Consider historical trends and market conditions to forecast future revenue.

3. Analyze your expenses: Categorize expenses into fixed (e.g., rent, salaries) and variable (e.g., supplies, advertising). Review expenses regularly to identify areas for cost reduction.

4. Set financial goals: Determine your financial objectives, such as increasing revenue, reducing expenses, or improving cash flow. Use these goals as a guide when creating your budget.

5. Allocate resources: Allocate resources based on your revenue and expense projections, focusing on essential expenses and investments that support your business goals.

6. Review and adjust: Regularly review your budget to ensure it remains accurate and relevant. Adjust your budget as needed to reflect changes in your business's financial situation or market conditions.

Remember, a budget is only useful if it is accurate and reflective of your business's financial situation. Be diligent in your tracking and forecasting to ensure your budget remains relevant and effective in helping you manage your business finances.

## Managing cash flow

Managing cash flow is critical to the success of any business, regardless of its size or industry. Cash flow refers to the amount of money that flows in and out of your business over a given period. Managing cash flow involves keeping track of the money that is coming into and going out of your business, and ensuring that you have enough cash on hand to cover your expenses.

Here are some tips for managing cash flow:

1. Create a cash flow statement: A cash flow statement will help you to understand your cash inflows and outflows. You can use this information to make better decisions about your business operations.

2. Monitor your accounts receivable: Your accounts receivable are the amounts owed to you by your customers. It's important to keep track of these accounts and follow up with customers who are slow to pay.

3. Manage your accounts payable: Your accounts payable are the amounts you owe to your suppliers and vendors. It's important to manage these accounts carefully and pay your bills on time to avoid late fees or interest charges.

4. Forecast your cash flow: Create a cash flow forecast for the coming weeks or months. This will help you to anticipate any cash shortages and take steps to prevent them.

5. Negotiate payment terms: Negotiate payment terms with your suppliers and customers to ensure that you have enough cash on hand to cover your expenses.

6. Keep a cash reserve: Maintain a cash reserve to cover unexpected expenses or to help you weather any downturns in your business.

7. Use accounting software: Use accounting software to help you track your cash inflows and outflows, and to create reports that will help you to manage your cash flow effectively.

By implementing these strategies, you can better manage your cash flow and ensure that your business remains financially stable.

# CHAPTER IX

# Hiring and Managing Employees

As your business grows, you may find that you need to hire employees to help you manage your workload. Hiring and managing employees can be a challenging task, but it is also an essential part of building a successful business. In this chapter, we will discuss the key steps involved in hiring and managing employees.

1. Develop a hiring plan

Before you start looking for employees, it's essential to develop a hiring plan. This plan should include the following:

- Job description: Clearly define the job responsibilities and requirements for the position you are hiring for.

- Qualifications: Identify the skills and qualifications that are necessary for the job.

- Compensation: Determine the salary or hourly wage that you are willing to pay for the position.

- Recruitment strategy: Decide how you will advertise the job opening and attract potential candidates.

- Interview process: Develop a list of questions that you will ask during the interview process to assess candidates' skills and fit for the position.

2. Advertise the job opening

Once you have developed a hiring plan, you need to advertise the job opening to attract potential candidates. There are several ways to do this, including:

- Posting the job opening on online job boards such as Indeed, LinkedIn, or Glassdoor.

- Advertising the job opening on your company's website and social media accounts.

- Networking with industry contacts and asking for referrals.

3. Interview candidates

After you have received applications from potential candidates, it's time to interview them. During the interview process, you should:

- Ask open-ended questions to get a sense of the candidate's experience and qualifications.

- Assess their communication and interpersonal skills.

- Discuss the job responsibilities and expectations to ensure that they are a good fit for the position.

4. Onboard new employees

Once you have hired a new employee, it's essential to onboard them properly to ensure that they are set up for success. This includes:

- Providing them with an orientation and introducing them to the company's culture and values.

- Providing them with the necessary tools and resources to perform their job effectively.

- Setting goals and expectations for their performance.

5. Manage employee performance

Managing employee performance is a critical part of ensuring that your business runs smoothly. To do this effectively, you should:

- Provide regular feedback and coaching to help employees improve their performance.

- Set clear goals and expectations for their performance.

- Conduct regular performance reviews to assess their progress and provide feedback.

6. Stay compliant with employment laws

Finally, it's essential to stay compliant with employment laws to avoid legal issues. This includes:

- Providing employees with the necessary benefits and compensation as required by law.

- Adhering to workplace safety regulations.

- Ensuring that your business is in compliance with employment discrimination laws.

By following these steps, you can hire and manage employees effectively, ensuring that your business runs smoothly and that your employees are set up for success

## When to hire employees

As a business owner, you may reach a point where you can no longer handle all the work on your own. This is a good indication that it's time to hire employees.

Here are some signs that you may need to bring in additional help:

1. You are turning down work because you don't have enough time to complete it all.

2. You are missing deadlines or struggling to keep up with the demands of your customers.

3. Your revenue has grown to the point where you can afford to hire someone.

4. You need to focus on tasks that require your expertise and delegate other tasks to someone else.

5. You are experiencing burnout and need to reduce your workload.

When considering hiring employees, it's important to assess your financial situation to ensure that you can afford to pay them. This includes not just their salary, but also additional expenses such as payroll taxes, benefits, and equipment or supplies needed for their work.

Once you've determined that you are ready to hire, it's important to develop a clear job description and requirements for the position. This will help you attract the right candidates and ensure that they have the necessary skills and experience.

Additionally, you will need to develop an onboarding process to ensure that your new employees are properly trained and integrated into your company culture. This may include providing them with a handbook that outlines your company policies and procedures, setting up training sessions, and assigning them a mentor or supervisor who can help them navigate their new role.

Finally, it's important to establish clear expectations and performance metrics for your employees, and to provide regular feedback and opportunities for professional development. This will help you build a strong and motivated team that can help your business grow and thrive.

## Tips for managing employees

Managing employees is a crucial part of running a successful business. Here are some tips to help you effectively manage your employees:

1. Hire the right people: Start by hiring the right people for the job. Look for individuals who have the necessary skills and experience, as

well as a positive attitude and a good work ethic.

2. Provide clear expectations: Be clear about what you expect from your employees, and communicate those expectations clearly. Make sure they know what their job duties are, how their performance will be measured, and what the consequences are for not meeting expectations.

3. Offer training and development: Provide your employees with training and development opportunities to help them improve their skills and knowledge. This can include on-the-job training, workshops, seminars, and online courses.

4. Provide feedback: Give your employees regular feedback on their performance. Let them know what they're doing well and where they need to improve. Use constructive feedback to help them grow and develop in their roles.

5. Recognize and reward good work: Recognize and reward your employees when they do a good job. This can include verbal praise, bonuses, promotions, or other forms of

recognition. It's important to show your employees that their hard work is valued and appreciated.

6. Address performance issues: If an employee is not meeting expectations, address the issue promptly. Be clear about what the issue is, and work with the employee to develop a plan to improve their performance.

7. Foster a positive work environment: Create a positive work environment where employees feel valued, supported, and respected. Encourage open communication, collaboration, and teamwork. Promote work-life balance and offer flexibility when possible.

By following these tips, you can effectively manage your employees and create a positive work environment that fosters growth and success.

## Cost-effective ways to hire

When it comes to hiring employees, it can be an expensive and time-consuming process. However, there are cost-effective ways to find and hire quality candidates for your business.

1. Utilize job posting sites: Instead of using traditional job boards or recruiters, consider posting job openings on job posting sites such as Indeed or ZipRecruiter. These sites have a broad reach and can attract a large pool of potential candidates.

2. Use social media: Social media platforms like LinkedIn, Facebook, and Twitter are great tools for reaching a wide audience. Post about job openings on your social media channels and encourage your followers to share the post to help spread the word.

3. Referral programs: Consider starting a referral program for your current employees. Offer incentives for referring quality candidates to the company. This not only encourages your employees to help with the hiring process, but it also helps ensure that new hires fit in with the company culture.

4. Internship programs: Consider offering internships to college students or recent graduates. This not only gives your company the opportunity to train and groom future

employees, but it also provides a cost-effective way to get extra help when needed.

5. Freelancers and contractors: Consider hiring freelancers or contractors for specific projects or tasks. This can be a cost-effective way to get the work done without the long-term commitment of hiring a full-time employee.

6. Use a staffing agency: If you are struggling to find quality candidates on your own, consider using a staffing agency. Staffing agencies can help with the hiring process and provide temporary employees as needed.

It's important to remember that hiring cost-effectively doesn't mean cutting corners. Taking the time to find quality candidates who fit your company culture and values is essential for long-term success.

# CHAPTER X
## Conclusion

In conclusion, growing a business on a budget requires careful planning, disciplined execution, and constant adaptation. It is essential to assess your current financial situation, create a realistic budget plan, and identify areas for improvement. Developing and implementing cost-effective marketing strategies, maximizing efficiency through streamlining operations, implementing technology, and outsourcing can help you reduce costs and increase revenue. When it comes to financing and funding options, you need to evaluate each option's pros and cons and choose the one that best fits your business needs.

As your business grows, you need to prepare for growth, scale your business while maintaining financial stability, and avoid common mistakes. Managing your business finances, including developing a budget and managing cash flow, is critical to ensure the long-term success of your business. Hiring and managing employees is another crucial aspect of business growth, and cost-effective ways to hire can help you save money while building a talented team.

Overall, growing a business on a budget requires careful planning, smart decisions, and hard work. It is a challenging journey, but with the right strategies, you can achieve your business goals and build a successful and sustainable business. Remember to regularly review and adjust your strategies to stay competitive and adapt to the changing market conditions. With these tips and guidance, you can take your business to the next level without breaking the bank.

## Recap of key points

Throughout this book, we have covered various aspects of growing a business on a budget. Here is a quick recap of the key points covered in each chapter:

Chapter I: Introduction to Growing a Business on a Budget

- Starting a business is a challenging task, and it becomes even more challenging when you have limited financial resources.

- However, it is possible to grow a business on a budget with careful planning, creative strategies, and a willingness to learn and adapt.

Chapter II: Assessing Your Current Finances

- Before you can create a budget or develop a growth plan, you need to have a clear understanding of your current financial situation.

- Evaluate your revenue, expenses, and profit margins to identify areas for improvement.

Chapter III: Creating a Budget

- A budget is a critical tool for managing your business finances and planning for growth.

- Create a realistic budget plan that considers all expenses, revenue streams, and financial goals.

Chapter IV: Marketing on a Budget

- Marketing is essential for reaching new customers and driving growth, but it can be expensive.

- Implement low-cost marketing strategies, such as social media marketing, content marketing, and referral marketing, to maximize your marketing impact on a limited budget.

## Chapter V: Maximizing Efficiency

- Streamlining operations and implementing technology can help reduce costs and increase productivity.

- Consider outsourcing certain tasks or functions to save on overhead costs.

## Chapter VI: Financing and Funding Options

- Explore different funding options, such as crowdfunding, grants, loans, venture capital, angel investors, and self-funding, to fund your business growth.

- Evaluate the pros and cons of each funding source and prepare a strong funding application to increase your chances of securing funding.

## Chapter VII: Scaling and Growth

- Preparing for growth is critical for successfully scaling your business.

- Develop a growth plan that considers your financial resources and identifies opportunities for growth while maintaining financial stability.

Chapter VIII: Managing Your Business Finances

- Managing your business finances is critical for achieving long-term success.

- Develop a budget and manage cash flow effectively to ensure financial stability and prepare for future growth.

Chapter IX: Hiring and Managing Employees

- Hiring and managing employees is a significant expense for many businesses, but it is necessary for growth and success.

- Consider cost-effective ways to hire and invest in employee training and development to increase productivity and performance.

In conclusion, growing a business on a budget is challenging but not impossible. By implementing the strategies and tips outlined in this book, you can achieve long-term success and growth for your business.

As we come to the end of this book, it's important to remember that the strategies and tips discussed here are only effective if put into action. Building a successful business on a budget requires determination, discipline, and the willingness to take risks.

Remember to regularly evaluate your financial situation and make adjustments to your budget as necessary. Utilize low-cost marketing strategies and efficient operations to maximize profits. Consider all funding options available to you and prepare strong applications to increase your chances of obtaining funding.

Scaling and growth can bring new challenges, but with proper planning and execution, it can lead to even greater success. Finally, when hiring and managing employees, focus on creating a positive and productive work environment.

Starting and growing a business on a budget is no easy feat, but it is possible. Believe in yourself and your vision, and don't be afraid to take calculated risks. With hard work and dedication, you can build a thriving business that is both financially stable and fulfilling.

## Final thoughts on growing a business without breaking the bank.

Growing a business on a budget is a challenging but rewarding task. It requires a lot of hard work, dedication, and creativity to find cost-effective solutions for different aspects of your business, including financing, marketing, operations, and hiring. However, by taking a strategic approach and leveraging different resources and tools, it is possible to grow your business without breaking the bank.

Throughout this book, we have discussed various strategies and best practices for growing a business on a budget. We have covered topics such as assessing your current financial situation, creating a realistic budget plan, marketing on a budget, maximizing efficiency, financing and funding options, and hiring and managing employees. By following these strategies and taking advantage of the different funding sources available to small businesses, you can position your business for growth and success.

It is important to remember that growing a business on a budget requires patience and persistence. It may take time to see the results of your efforts, but with dedication and hard work, success is possible. So, if you are ready to take your business to the next level, use the information and strategies in this book to create a roadmap for success. Remember, the key is to stay focused on your goals and to always be willing to adapt and make changes as necessary to achieve them.

"Growing Your Business Without Breaking the Bank: Proven Strategies for Maximizing Growth on a Budget for all Businesses" is a comprehensive guide to help entrepreneurs and small business owners grow their businesses without draining their finances. The book is designed to provide practical tips and strategies to help businesses increase revenue, reduce expenses, and effectively manage their finances to support growth.

The book covers a wide range of topics, including assessing your current finances, creating a realistic budget plan, marketing on a budget, maximizing efficiency, financing and funding options, scaling and growth, and managing your business finances. Each chapter is packed with actionable advice, real-life examples, and helpful resources to help readers implement the strategies covered.

Whether you are just starting out or looking to take your business to the next level, "Growing Your Business Without Breaking the Bank" provides valuable insights and tools to help you achieve your goals without sacrificing financial stability. With this book as a guide, entrepreneurs and small business owners can confidently navigate the challenges of growing their businesses while keeping their finances in check.

# ABOUT THE AUTHOR

**Bamidele Iseoluwa Nathaniel** is a multi-talented individual with a passion for technology, finance, and writing. With a background in software engineering, web development, Affiliate Marketing, and graphics design, Bamidele is a skilled professional in the tech field. As a co-founder of **Agromerce International Limited Company**, also in partnership with **Waplia Digital Solutions (a private limited company in India)**. Bamidele has demonstrated his entrepreneurial spirit and business acumen.

In addition to his technical expertise, Bamidele is also an avid trader in forex and cryptocurrency, demonstrating a keen understanding of financial markets. However, perhaps most noteworthy is Bamidele's dedication to his faith, which is a central part of his life and values.

Bamidele's diverse interests and experiences make him a unique and valuable voice in the world of writing. With his passion for technology, finance, and faith, Bamidele brings a unique perspective to the subject of ***"Growing Your Business Without Breaking the Bank: Proven Strategies for Maximizing Growth on a Budget for all Businesses"***. We are excited to see what Bamidele will accomplish in his future endeavors as a writer.


*Thanks for reading*